Vincent van Gogh

Vincent van Gogh

by Eileen Lucas
illustrations by Rochelle Draper

Carolrhoda Books, Inc./Minneapolis

This book is available in two editions:
Library binding by Carolrhoda Books, Inc.
Soft cover by First Avenue Editions
c/o The Lerner Publishing Group
241 First Avenue North, Minneapolis, MN 55401 U.S.A.

Library of Congress Cataloging-in-Publication Data

Lucas, Eileen.
  Vincent van Gogh / by Eileen Lucas ; illustrations by
Rochelle Draper.
    p. cm. — (Carolrhoda on my own books)
  Summary: Follows the life and artistic development of
the painter who moved from Belgium and Holland to
France, was influenced by Impressionism, and
eventually created his own unique style.
  ISBN 1-57505-038-2 (lib. bdg.)
  ISBN 1-57505-062-5 (pbk.)
  1. Gogh, Vincent van, 1853–1890—Juvenile literature.
2. Painters—Netherlands—Biography—Juvenile
literature. [1. Gogh, Vincent van, 1853–1890. 2. Artists.
3. Painting, Dutch. 4. Painting, Modern—19th
century—Netherlands. 5. Art appreciation.] I. Draper,
Rochelle, 1960–   ill. II. Title. III. Series.
ND653.G7L755 1997
759.9492—dc20
[B]   96-27617

Manufactured in the United States of America
1 2 3 4 5 6 – JR – 02 01 00 99 98 97

Holland
May 1885

One evening Vincent van Gogh
watched a family sit down
for dinner.
It was dark in their small house.
Their only food was
a plate of potatoes.
Vincent didn't share their meal.
He was there to draw them.

For five years,
Vincent had been working as an artist.
He had begun by using pencils
and charcoal sticks.
He drew the farmers and weavers
who lived and worked around him.

Most of these people were poor,
and their lives were hard.
It showed in their faces and
in their hands.
Vincent made it show
in his drawings too.
As he grew more skilled,
Vincent began to use oil paints.

Now he wanted to paint
the family eating potatoes.
For months, Vincent worked
on this painting.
Mostly he used very dark greens
and browns.
The one bright spot was the yellow
in the oil lamp over the table.

When it was finally finished,

he sent it to his brother, Theo.

Theo lived in Paris, France.

He worked in a gallery,

a place that sold paintings.

He tried to sell the pictures

Vincent sent him.

But no one seemed to want to buy

Vincent's pictures.

Still, every week or so,
Theo sent Vincent some money.
Then Vincent could buy art supplies.
He could pay the rent for the place
he lived in.
If there was any money left,
he could buy food.

Often, Vincent had only bread
and potatoes to eat.
Sometimes he had nothing
to eat at all.
As a result, he was often
weak and sick.
But he would not give up.
"I shall do what I can.
I shall work hard," he wrote to Theo.

Vincent wrote many letters to Theo.

Sometimes he added small pictures

to his letters.

Theo also wrote to Vincent.

He told Vincent about some painters

who lived in Paris.

They were called impressionists.

Their paintings were filled with light and with bright colors.
They used short, quick brush strokes.
They tried to paint an impression, or idea, of what they saw.
Vincent decided it was time to see those paintings for himself.

Paris, France
February 1886

A messenger gave Theo a note.
It was from Vincent.
He was waiting for Theo
at an art museum in Paris.
Theo went to meet his brother.
Right away, he invited Vincent
to live with him.

Theo was four years younger
than Vincent, but he often acted
like the older brother.
He soon sent Vincent to
a dentist and a doctor.
Theo wrote to their mother,
"I think his difficult times are over."

But Vincent was not an easy person
to get along with.
He argued with everyone,
even the people he cared about most.
When he was angry he shouted.
And he got angry a lot.
Sometimes he would yell at people
in a mixture of Dutch, English,
and French!

He stayed out late at night.

He made a mess of Theo's apartment
with his clothes and his paints.

"He makes life hard," wrote Theo.

But he loved Vincent.

And Vincent loved him.

While Vincent was in Paris,
he met many painters.
He ate and drank and talked
with them in the cafés.
He painted outside with them
under the blue skies of Paris.
He loved to paint outside!
He loved to see the colors of nature
come alive in the sun.

Vincent began to use
these bright colors in his paintings.
He squirted the paint
from little tubes onto his palette.
There were pinks and reds and violets
for flowers.
There were many shades of blue
for the sky.
And there was yellow for the sun.

Vincent lived in Paris for two years.
He learned a great deal
from other painters there.
But he wanted to work on
his own way to paint.
He decided to go south,
where there would be more sun
for light and warmth.

He left a painting on an easel
in his room, hoping that Theo
would not be lonely.
He left many of his other paintings
hanging on the walls.
Then he took a train
to the south of France.

Arles, France
February 1888

It was cold in Arles

and there was snow on the ground.

But Vincent was happy to be

in this place.

He found an inn

where he could eat and sleep.

Then he went to work.

"Here I am seeing new things.

I am learning," he wrote to Theo.

25

Soon the sun came out
and melted all the snow.
Then a strong cold wind
called the mistral began to blow.
But Vincent wanted to paint
the fruit trees that were in bloom.

While the wind shook his canvas,
he kept on painting.
Even when the wind knocked
the canvas down,
he did not quit.
He left the canvas on the ground
and painted on his knees.

27

Vincent used bright and
brighter colors.
Sometimes he squeezed paint
right from the tubes onto his picture.
He put the paint on thick
and left it that way.
Ridges and lines of thick paint
covered his work.
Sometimes his paintings took weeks
to dry because there was so much
paint on them!

As spring moved into summer,
Vincent kept on painting.
When the hot afternoon sun
burned brightly in the sky,
most people looked for
a cool place to rest.
But not Vincent.

He stood in the golden fields of wheat
and painted them.
He painted a yellow bridge
against a bright blue sky.
He painted women washing clothes
in the river.
He painted the farmers' cottages
with their red roofs.

Day after day he painted.
When the sun burned the top of his
red head, he put on a straw hat
and kept painting.
He did not care that the blazing sun
could make him sick.
The sun made everything brighter,
and Vincent loved it.

Even when it grew dark,
Vincent did not stop.
He just stuck candles in his hat
and kept on painting!
He chose purples, blues, and greens
to show the colors of the night.
He used yellow for the stars and
lanterns that took the place of the sun.

Vincent must have looked strange
to the people of Arles.
He carried his painting things
on his back.
His clothes were wrinkled
and covered with paint.
His red hair was likely to be
standing up in all directions.
He liked to run his fingers through it
when he got excited.

Vincent saw so much to paint.
He wanted to paint it all right away.
One of his great works, *The Harvest*,
was painted in a single day.
He was afraid people would think
he worked too fast.
But he said he had to work quickly,
"just like the harvester."

Vincent soon became tired of
living at the inn.
He needed a place to work
when the weather was bad.
So he found a house
that was just right for him.
It was a yellow house—
the color of the sun,
the color of stars and lanterns.

He bought a bed and some chairs.
Then he painted a picture
of his bedroom.
He made pictures of sunflowers
to hang on the walls.
They were bright yellow like the sun.
Vincent loved to look at them.

Vincent invited another painter,
Paul Gauguin, to visit him there.
He dreamed of filling the little house
with painters at work.

At the end of October,
Paul came to Arles.
For two months, the artists
worked together in the yellow house.

But Vincent wasn't taking
very good care of himself.
He didn't eat well
and he worked too hard.
He was very tired,
but he did not rest.
He argued and fought
with Paul Gauguin.
After one terrible fight,
Paul decided to leave Arles.
Vincent was very ill
and could not think straight.
He went to a mental hospital,
where people could take care of him.
Sometimes he got very upset,
or very sad.
During these times,
he could not paint.

But when he felt better,
all he wanted to do was paint.
And then he painted some
very beautiful pictures.

One of these is called
The Starry Night.
It shows a nighttime sky
that is bright with swirling light.
One time Vincent said,
"Looking at the stars
always makes me dream."

Vincent had found a style
of his own.
He had shown his feelings
in his paintings.
He had found new ways
to use color and paint.
But he could not find a way
to get better.
He was too sick and too tired.
Nothing, it seemed, could cure him.

Vincent was only thirty-seven
when he died.
His brother and his friends
put yellow flowers on his coffin.
They looked at the many paintings
that Vincent had made.
In the sun and the stars
in his paintings,
Vincent van Gogh would live on.

Self-Portrait *(1889)*
by Vincent van Gogh

Afterword

When Vincent died, Theo was very sad. He became very ill and died six months later. Theo's wife, Johanna, knew how much the brothers cared about each other. She saw to it that they were buried next to each other. She also saved all the letters that they had written to each other, and all the paintings and drawings that Vincent had given to Theo. The letters were published in books, and the paintings were shown in galleries and museums all over the world.

In ten short years, Vincent had painted hundreds of pictures—over two hundred while he lived in Paris and two hundred more while he lived in Arles. Though Vincent sold only one painting during his lifetime, people now pay millions of dollars for a painting by Vincent van Gogh.

Important Dates

March 30, 1853—Vincent van Gogh was born in Zundert, Holland.

1873–1876—Worked at art galleries in London and Paris

1878–1879—Became a preacher and worked in Belgium

1880—Decided to become an artist; gained brother Theo's support

1880–1886—Improved skills as artist while living in Belgium and Holland

May 1885—Painted *The Potato Eaters*

February 1886—Arrived in Paris, France

February 1888—Moved to Arles, France

December 1888—Entered a hospital in Arles

May 1889—Entered a mental hospital in St. Rémy, France

June 1889—Painted *The Starry Night*

May 1890—Moved to Auvers, France

July 29, 1890—Died in Auvers